ANNUNCIATION SONNETS

Also by Linda Kemp

CONTENTS

ISBN: 978-1-916938-09-0

Cover designed by Aaron Kent

Edited and Typeset by Aaron Kent

Broken Sleep Books Ltd
PO BOX 102
Llandysul
SA44 9BG

Annunciation Sonnets

Linda Kemp

Broken Sleep Books

fra angelico

unadorned humility
the psychological state of posture
written in
gesture
the quietude of conversation
standing to
so the surrounding question
prepares

the gesture of a martyr is no place marker
the feast sleeps on
the dirt of the street
lays to meet
the rising

triumphal arch, santa maria maggiore

scented recognition dedicates following
to beg-
      inning   a stylistic error under-
      written   the earliest extant image
wrought in the form of a dove
           do not doubt promise
           marriage
the fall of snow
                in all rich pontifications
of champagne dénouement
selling property on a social justice ticket
      academicians
                  rot the covenant
to debate

[   ]

the reassembling of a grief-torn city
the many rooms of my father

below the massacre of innocents
the massacre of poets   speakers of
quietude   of grief
the luminosity of circles
the high-backed chair of damage
                        three intercessions
leave the road this way
                            mosaics breaking
rendering   arriving   a counterpart
            to debate the reason   to know
            discourse discontent

triumphal arch, santa maria maggiore (ii)

speakers on burning
       roofs
the sybil below a beatrice registers
another millbank
another tony b
       (-enn, not b
       -lair)   accustoming
the wash of flame & hell-
ishness of futures with
out hope   hanging in the hands of
that other blake
bonney
breathes   the dove
       enters through lips

bernardo daddi

presuming glory in the moment ends
often mysterious & emphasising
rioting as holy orders
                    the restoration of today
            variegates distinct decorate mediums

blunts scenes from screens to life
            but tiktok chastises

            the dialectic of propaganda
a moment
the oil on wood   clothed in gold
drip over honey
the insistence of extraordinary

hans memling

descent includes extra   the reminder
heresies express   the invisible
devotion to   feasting destruction of
an establishment lucky to live in such a terrible age
the destitute dying in get-rich-quick cities
     the meeting at the golden gate
     the unlucky bridge   the garden
passageway to
alleluia
the council of ephesus   look out
look out
the swirling & jaunty promises of graduation degrade
     a mourning diary
     an enclosed order

refectory relief (priory of cluny)

        nimbed, so it seems
alternative with nothing the nowhere
of each citizen
clamped into subject
the beatings of
        witness as a form of dignity
failing
in capitals

parliamentarians shiver
in the river   blake's prophecies
beard out   correct
genuflect at the crossroads
relief in the rail

[   ]

vomit composition
              the event likens the womb to the ear
              the slight stain of the
memorial window
              the silence of remote parish churches
              the unbelieving of the graphic
              passing of gagging
legislative orders to bound up the un-
bounded joy of boundlessness
                     beneath elaborate identities
              a meme
              the wheat-field without wheat but a woman
              running in rebellion
                     feeding none

[   ]

listen   daughter
           incline & in your ear
           the precipitous
           dive
to a missive waiting & waits
& rarely attributes the passing ear
the entry to origins
           beginning with enunciation
submission is the beginning of intimate
           knowing
           the barricades hold babies
& the previous marriage
folds
           to show

arbor vitae

a lavish of gold leaf
reversal gilded
alliance   specifically the scenes of marriage
& inclusion
              the desiring source
illuminator of curling fruit
                        on twelve branches
the pelican rips
a fire sanctifying the mind
              virtue of the formed   creating
in the forming
              characteristics light
              the infrequency of conception
influencing popularity with a start

the master of the netze, marienthal

the appearance of the body
before the body
            suggests a function   a prescribing
behaviour looking sharply
                    contrary to objection   the body
grows   the appearance of the child
finally condemned   a citation an
accreditation of the first definition of capitalism
the score   mercers   goldsmiths
against the representation of midwives
lives in the original latin translate   that is
the actual source of light
            the source of sacrifice
opening an east-facing window   facing

lippo vanni

materialisation divides in sincerity   the
          sensitive descent towards the
heel   the status of event
patterned   vaults frame a surround the
design cut

                  through
          no doubt   below the prisoners
the freely roaming rights of righteousness
the opposite of celibate
the angles of illumination
          recess   the possibility of revolution
wiping design from her face
sorrow is the swathes of substance stanning
robes

biagio di goro ghezzi

striking the expanded sounds a prominence
       a way to act the hospital
in exterior walls   the decorated acts
cycling through interiority   the scales
of circular saws standing about prophetic apses
       either side of fore intimacies
       stand ashore
to tear the entrance over
         the famous the famed the
good looks of looking slowly
sourcing the visible from whosoever believes

         your name is long forgotten
         did   do something wrong

[the angel kneels]

a bench a little terrace a
rug   lush with fidget toys   the invisible
lake drained long ago   who goes
here without reason goes
chronic & characteristic of
          mirrors wrapping careers as though
these are reasons   the rational
thumb sucking of winning
          that tunnel wind forces
          back the origins
the wrong of claiming nothing for the losing
way of knowing
                    what is wrong & waking it
patronage is wooded landscape   a holy &

fra filippo lippi

                            the glass tips

wings of waiting

            independently suffocating in-

dependency & composition   the visibility of no

windows   the wall the cupboard

doors   the way to wake the liturgical silver

the tongue of knowing to satiate

            from the window the egg

            a fictive frame of

familiarity bows to scepticism   the wide

worlds of water in vessels

            the favourite produce of florence

florida   the fathers bursting with

burst incantations   that infrequent vase

gentile da fabriano

influential metaphors steep in imagination
       the proselytising preacher sleeping
undoubting mouths
              views are dampened
allegories   the wide flesh finished
the reconfiguration of all parts parted
       the device is inspired
       the word of painting
assumed dead &
            clothed heavenwards   except
below
       in the dark recesses of inbox incantations
the failure of finding
the luminous energy   in composition

andrea della robbia

at the reading desk
the reading sees the lily
      speech
      is crown
self-serving & stuffy
despite tottering to doctors daily
to seep
to pots glazed & left
      shrines
this path treads jewels
history economising
the decoration of staying
away   rebuilding emblems
a source as cue for doubt

rogier van der weyden

withdrawn to the innermost striking
a startling customary
smile pelmeted   over the bed curtains
associating with reminiscence   the quails
& in absolute the scene
stumbles
recognisable through contemporaries
whose witness necessitates naturalistic
        stakes observed &
comfortable in illumination
                    switch to familiar objects & the background
owes consciousness
a fashionable perspective for a moment
prone to estrangement

jan van eyck

in this through this
        well-appointed knowing not to
point to
             status   the raising
             depicting two
picking out a puppy
& one pronoun

        in this book the pious
        objects
        marry objects
        the source of saving
undoing
        looks at comfort

master of aix

respectful distance remains unknown
a painting dismembered in remembrance
          identity torn in
          oblivious influence
the earth evidently cross &
a fistful of years
rows through portraiture as subject
                    whereabouts is reminiscence
          the backseat driving of
apprentices   it is obvious
to be dismembered on the left is an honour-
able sacrifice
to save face is to remember recent arrangements
the loss of brilliance   & lips

master of aix (ii)

countenance organises the familiar
settles into quoting parallel events
            to disprove occupation
the seating arrangements dissatisfactory
            resetting patrons to
beginnings
                        the hold separate
the tree & bird   the body
aware of dividing   & the symptoms
too dangerous to name in public
                        approving private disapproval
does not go quietly
the painting alters patiently   adapting
            resemblance to celebrate

giotto

directives of drama construct the choir
       to begin the curtains
chants whether the dawning
compartmentalisation   the existing
acting out above what acts out below
       a stationary working out
vested in oratory sanctification
       the dust bowl of
specificity   the necessarily linked charms
private & surrounded   roll up
the shown are each
       right angles to the body
that niche of decorative song
       between

[   ]

working the spindle is derisory
       the long-held belief of phds as
       keys to a long & happy labour
spurt blood across exteriors   the wooden
       smile of beasts in a garden
       the oral tradition of rectitude
the broken sphincter of trying too hard
those various discrepancies around the middle
       shrines to destroyed childhoods

the first documentation of salutation
       drips in purple in hands
with relative ease & conversation
the lesser-known & less influential held

nicholas of verdun

transmitting the moment to ear
taught nothing
       the central row above
the law the goldsmith inscribed
            the gilded frame
absolute certainty consists for precious
compartmentalisation
figureheads
the promise of power a plaque below
the recluse pronouncing
portable moments of enduring strangers
      encouragement harnesses
moments of regularity
      a ticking

johann von soest

niches of solitude
        result of volume   the spent
treatise a respectability   the recommended
piousness of fathers
looks down the   a valuable object
squats &
                 in the forefinger of society
permits devotion
        reoccurrence is bodily
        the silence slews
a contemplation
                 a chef's seclusion
attends to the desk
availability a lectern

footnote: the role of the angel

close relationship is given
          in praise
in days gone scholars longed on
style   the grounds of
acceptance   allusion
the mystery of citation
unblocking veneration with a ghost
          whatsapp & assorted idols
blocked in
          the dissociated   an in-
ability to think the schedule through
thrice
          praise is punitive
          praise heads up the streets

simone martini

potency troubles

        shimmering wings surround the poised
the listening mouth
turned down the folded salutation
            to dwell in rumours
      solicits the delicate finesse of
      finitude the training of leaves
to wither in the mind as
only narrative on the northern side &
poets queue to the east
            reconstruction in doubt
exalts collaboration
      continually clear

[   ]

adoption parallels
            unsure of worth the certain
hold to significance
the quaint wail of trouble the
eventfulness of counsel
the man who can never quite
                    anonymity is a shirt
        the shadow of saving
        exactitude for awkwardness
fragility & diffidence   the upturning
how   to be so
                    perhaps in this
to be behind pillars
the poor & the reversal beyond

giotto, again

silence greets the welcome
each room a delivery
       in categorisation
slips significance
            the willing wildness
bewildering piety as exercise
      to bend in
notice what should have been said
partially &
the many show an interest
            an exchange
between agitation & display   but decorum
in the error
by shock

Acknowledgements

The sections beginning "the reassembling of a grief-torn city" and "vomit composition" first appeared in *Datableed* #14. Thanks to the editors at *Datableed*.

LAY OUT YOUR UNREST